Tails, trails,

and Campfire stories

Photographs, Poetry And musings
Of an Alberta farm girl

SHERRY SIKSTROM

Order this book online at www.trafford.com
or email orders@trafford.com

Most Trafford titles are also available at major online book retailers.

Printed in the United States of America.

ISBN: 978-1-4669-1476-6 (sc)
978-1-4669-1475-9 (e)

Library of Congress Control Number: 2012902317

Trafford rev. 03/17/2012

 www.trafford.com

North America & international
toll-free: 1 888 232 4444 (USA & Canada)
phone: 250 383 6864 ♦ fax: 812 355 4082

Tails, trails, and Campfire stories

Photographs, Poetry

And musings

Of an Alberta farm girl

By

Sherry Sikstrom

Of Fern Valley Appaloosas

This, my second book, is dedicated first to my wonderful and supportive family, and friend's .Your love and support make me believe anything is possible! And of course to the beautiful creatures large and small who continue to grace my life

"If it is possible, I will do it .If it is impossible, it will take me a little longer" Author unknown

I read this quote several years ago. And it spoke to me in its simplicity, and clear determination. This phrase defines the people in my life who were and are my heroes and the people I am proud to call family.

From my great grandfather William Horricks who settled on the old homestead near Edmonton and proceeded to build a life with his family, to my Grandfather George Horricks , who with his brother Charlie built and established Horricks Dairy , a formidable entity in its own right from 1927 to 1977.

Initially delivering milk to customers with horse and wagon, then in later years more modern modes. George served on the board of directors and as president of the Alberta Dairy Pool. Charlie, a blacksmith, of note, as he had only one arm as a result of a motor vehicle accident, and George, who also due to injury, had lost his hand, were two of the most able and capable men I have ever known! Teaching me that nothing is impossible, it just takes some "figuring".

The farm continued with the growing partnership of George and his sons. Bud (Milton) Bill and Ron. They worked not only in the dairy, but in a large commercial cattle operation as well as grain farming.

This is where I grew up, and found my enduring love of animals and the land. And where I learned a work ethic, about family, loyalty and love.

The first "real job" I held was at the age of 10 washing bottles and delivering milk on the farm. I was so proud of the cheques I received from Grandpa!

The bottles I delivered were plain, but the original Horricks Dairy bottles looked like this.

The Label Read
Horricks Dairy
"Natural Milk, Naturally the best"
A phrase coined by my grandfather.

My love of literature, and knowledge came also from my Granddad Blaine; he was an avid reader and shared his love of literature with us all. Again not one to let adversity slow him down, he returned to High school at the age of 42 completed his Grade 12 Matriculation!

I have kept the lessons of these heroes close to my heart, all of my life. At the age of 18 I moved away from the family farm to start my life on the ranch near Onoway. Caring for the stock and attending college to study Animal Health Technology. My path changed, as they often do and I found a career in Health care, working first with adult survivors of brain injury , then later as I expanded my knowledge in health care as a Home support aid and finally as a Mental Health aide , providing support to individuals in my community .

Through all of this I have maintained a breeding operation of the beautiful Appaloosas horses I adore, as well raising beef cattle; first with my dad, and now with my husband Martin , whose support and encouragement for my writing has been outstanding .

My poetry is written, always from the heart, and about the life I live here at Fern Valley; about and for the wonderful people and animals who have been part of my life.

<u>Remembering</u>

This first selection of poems is homage to my family and proud heritage. "Remembering Home", a reminiscence of a magical time and place in my life. "The Star in My Eyes" written for my father, who has been a mentor and hero to me always. "I will remember you Laughing" is a bittersweet farewell to a beloved Uncle.

Remembering Home

Dusty and Jigs, and an old dog named Peps
And grabbing the paper, off Aunties Barbs steps
Awaiting the School bus by the highway in September
Just some of the times I still can remember
The big old Spruce trees that reach for the sky
One lit up for Christmas in all years gone by

The old Dairy barn
And salt in blue blocks
This is the place, where I learned to walk
And to work and to ride, both bikes and on horses
And learned the true facts
Of Nature's good and bad forces
Delivering milk, all round the farm
Those crates seemed so heavy, upon my young arm

The sweet smell of silage that wrinkled your nose
And the wonderful feeling of grass on your toes
Sweet peas so fragrant all up on the vine
Scented the breeze near grandmas clothesline
Our gardens so huge and us on our knees
Griping and grumbling
Picking green beans and peas
Farm life is good it isn't all hard
I remember the water fights out in the big yard

100 years plus, here on this land
Where a young William Horricks. First took a stand
A heritage built, on hard work and grit

Where all of us learned, to just never quit
With George, and with Charlie, then Bud, Bill and Ron
They took up the torch, the old place stood strong

And now progress has come,
As we knew that it would
Soon new homes will be built
Where our heritage stood
I wonder will they know
Will they understand?
The magic that lies right here in this land
The light of our dreams let loose to soar
The echo of cows and the big combines roar

The things I shall take, as I say farewell
To this space
Are the memories fond, and no matter the place
That each of us land, and wherever we roam
We learned it here first
Our family is home

The Star in my Eyes

He is somebody,
Not one of the guys
My own darling father
The star in my eyes

A farmer a mechanic and more, does it all
A true Good Samaritan, who will answer the call
Of help for a neighbor, family or friend
Or even a stranger a hand he will lend

From the time we were born,
Till we walked down the aisle And he gave us away,
Through tears and a smile
His daughter's knew It took only a call
And he would come running
And not let us fall

And now we are grown,
And well on our way
Yet not far, from our thoughts
or hearts does he stray

For this is the man, who raised us up right
Who dried our tears, late in the night
And kept us safe, in the circle of his arms
Until it was time, to let us take flight

And still even now, if troubles befall
We know he will be there, it just takes a call

So what do you give a man of such heart?
Somehow a card doesn't even start
To tell him how much he means and has done
Really, a gift? Why stop at just one

He has given so much
Ask none in return
how do you celebrate a light,

That so brightly burns?

Today of all days, I must at least try
Happy Birthday, to you
Dad you're a star in my eyes!

"I will remember you laughing"

I remember you laughing with total abandon
A wonderful memory I often reflect on
So much more to say and remember
The soul of a poet, a heart oh so tender

Square dancing or ballroom you fit in just fine
Then out to the fields and on the combine

Community minded, with an adventurous spirit
Climbing a windmill, with no sign you fear it
You took on the world and had a good look,
And saw so much more than is found in a book

Father, a husband, a brother and friend
A grandfather and uncle loved beyond end

And if you must leave us and go on ahead
We will have memories to hold in your stead
Save us a place, and wait for us there
And oh! One day, the stories we'll share

But in the meanwhile
As time keeps on passing
In my heart and my mind
I will remember you laughing

Tails and trails

This selection is to celebrate the joys of some of the wonderful horses and pets who I have loved.

Their stories and a few of mine

<u>Trails will end</u>

The day comes to us all of course
We can no longer ride a horse
While I hope and I do humbly pray
That day is still yet, years away
I will not face that time with tears
Or bitterness regrets and fears
The retirement that I have earned
Will be time to share what I have learned
And hope some young and open mind
Will take up the trails left behind
So on that day some time from now
When I chase that one last cow
Or ride out into the bright blue day
I will celebrate it in my way
And step down one last time with grace
And with contentment look on the face
Of one who's heart has been true and strong
And carried me for oh so long
Whatever horse it may be,
In their gentle eyes I will see
All of them that came before
I dare not ask for any more

The Pistol

In my youth,
I knew a horse
Satan, was his name
To tell the truth
It isn't fair
He was mostly
Pretty tame
Easy to catch
More often than not
And he stood
Just where you tied him
He wasn't really all that hot
Until
You tried to ride him

<u>A Wish</u>

A wish, whispered in a grey mare's ear
The waiting began for nearly a year
Would she be equal to the task?
If you knew Schiroc, You wouldn't ask
On an August morn so bright
There he was, both black and white
A handsome boy, a win it's clear
With lightning bolts upon each ear

He grew up loved and kind and loyal
With a little thought that he was royal
The "little Prince "was kind and true
Blue Ebony, but we just called him Blue
Steady, quiet, gentle and sane
A horse that was chosen again and again
A horse like that, can't be replaced
And touched every life he graced
As we said good bye, through our tears
We whisper in a grey mare's ear

Learning to live

When training a horse
Here is a secret I have learned
More often than not
The tables are turned
While we go along
Thinking we are teaching
The horse goes along with
What we are preaching
But look a bit deeper
And you see a surprise
The very best teacher
Resides in their eyes
We ask them to give, to lead on a line
They teach us of patience, respect and of time
We get on their backs, as really we must
They show us the ultimate form of trust
We teach about pressure, contact and release
They show us their honesty, and willingness to please
We push them and try them and ask them to give
Give us all that and
They teach us to live

Once upon a Trail ride

Once upon a trail ride
I rode across a meadow wide
I met a young man on that trail
Full of boastful stories and tails
He talked about his big black horse
Fastest thing on feet of course
I rode along and listened some
And though 'bout how his day would come
He started then to joke and spin
"Your horse can't catch her second wind!"
The horse I rode was long and lank,
I knew just what she had in her tank
I shrugged and smile and rode away
But he kept at me the whole day.
Finally I gave in. And
Said alright
Let's take a spin
Along an open trail we ran
Neck and neck along the sand
That black horse ran with all his heart
Until I asked, when do we start?

Rich and Lucky

You'll get rich and I'll get lucky
now there is a place to start!
Those words were spoken by none other
than the man who took my heart
now wait a bit,
don't let your mind go down those sullied courses
the conversation was nothing wrong,
quite simply about horses
Get Rich Quick, and Lucky Chant,
were 2 good mares you see
He made a deal when we met
and bought them both for me.
Not a common courtship really,
he didn't bring me roses
Instead, he brought a cow and calf,
and horses with soft noses
But knowing me as I do, I think he had insight
A guy who brings his girl livestock
In my book gets it right!
Roses fade and chocolates spoil,
nothing lasts forever
but raising horses, and raising cows
Is what we do together

Think of Me

Think of me, now and then
take the time, remember when
I was the brightest light you saw
When you dreamed of me with awe
I was there first ,in your heart
then you grew up and we did part
On to bigger brighter ways
But oh how I miss those days
When you called me first
And I would run,
straight to you
my days of sun
As we learned and as we grew
and across those open fields we flew
The joys that we shared together
I thought they would last forever
You loved me first , And I you
what great things we did do
For now I will patiently wait,
Until I see you at the gate
and to you my soft ear will bend,
so think of me , now and then

Waiting

Though the spring seems far away
I eagerly await the day
When my good mares begin to show
The foal is due, after winter's snow
I watch and wait
Checking often
To see the signs my heart will soften
Then often in the early morn
Another beauty will be born
On wobbly legs they take their start

And wind their way into my heart
As they grow up strong and tall
On the pasture into the fall
I watch them with a loving eye
And dream of their futures flying high
Yup these babies make me happy
For who wouldn't love a Fern Valley Appy

A good dog

While moving cows one chilly night
I found myself in quite a plight
Our two young bulls did take a chance
And began to dance an age old dance
They were not really after me
I just got in the way you see
As I looked round for a line of flight
My hero arrived in black and white
He nipped and danced and barked and charged
And those two bulls although so large
Parted quick and went on their way
To quietly go eat their hay
Some will read this with surprise
As this dog can be a bit unwise
He is shy and silly often times

And has gotten into awful binds
But when it comes to cows
You see
He is fast and brave
And that works for me

Winston

A big yellow guy
With love in his eyes
He will turn doubters into believers
Loyal and kind
And gentle of mind
Winston, the Golden Retriever
A friend and a greeter
And savior of Skeeter
His little buddy, he protects,
From coyotes, and thunder
And wide eyed wonder
For all of the thanks that he gets
Under the watchful eye

Of this wonderful guy

Farm babies of

All kinds are guarded

He puts up with lots

From all kinds of tots

And has never

Become hard hearted

Hours he did log

As therapy dog

A task he excelled

And well worth it

At the end of the day

What more can I say

He is practically freakin

Perfect

Campfire Stories and other "truths"

Sometimes around the table or campfire, stories are told. Now everyone knows that campfire stories grow and become much more exciting with every telling. But they are all true! Right?

Guys like that

A farmer and cowboy
A hunter and such
You could tell to look at
Him he didn't eat much
A burger and some whiskey
He will never tire
A guy like that's built
Out of old baling wire
Tall lean and lanky
With a fist like a mitt.
Call him out when he is drinking
And he will get into it!
A jab or a punch, and
Down on the ground
He will give it his all
On every go round
But tell him his friend
Has got in a bind
He will stop in an instant
And leave it behind
He will show up to help
And bring long a crew
And whatever you need,
Well that's what he'll do
They don't make them quite
Like that anymore
But the ones that are here,
Are good ones for sure

The Shortcut Appy

Let me tell you a story from some time ago
From the days when away I would go
Out to the "hills" with my good horse and ride
Inspired by the beautiful Mountain side.

I rode with good folks, family and such
To make them all laugh, just didn't take much

We rode in the rain, the weather was crappy
and I rode along on "The Short cut Appy"
Not really her name, but a title she earned
a wonderful horse, with power to burn

We rode along a ridge one day as a bunch
and then it happened, just before lunch

The group got ahead at the top of a climb
Catana, and I, had fallen behind
I looked up to see riders above me
and away we did go! Oh heaven does love me

In 5 mighty leaps she went up the side
Grabbing leather and mane I went for a ride!
She made it alright and took me with her

but I do have to say, I wasn't all sure

She made that steep climb,
and she made it snappy

from then she was known as
"the Short Cut Appy"

Back at the camp the story was told
and jokes were many as the evening got old
No one was worried 'bout a fall or a bruise
But I heard them all yell
"Don't drop the booze!"

Jim& Duke

I have heard the boys sit and talk
About a guy, his name Jim Stock
And Duke his red roan horse
This story has no happy ending
But must be told of course
He rode that horse into the bars
And raced alongside railway cars
The second though it wasn't wise
And brought about old Dukes demise
One cold morn before the sun
Against the train a race was run
Galloped free along the frost
Until that tragic race was lost
There is no way to make it pretty
The horse died there, and mores the pity
Sadly Jim too died young
So many songs left unsung
But in the sound of distant thunder
Could we all take pause and wonder?
If the rumble in the clouds and rain
Are Jim and Duke Racing
Trains

Campfire Stories

Sit and listen to the guys
Tell their tales
And tell their lies
Revisiting the
Youthful glories
Disguising them in
Campfire stories
As the nights grow late and old
The bigger stories now are told
The fish, the bear, the 10 point buck
The day they nearly rolled the truck
Faster horses bigger climbs
As they relive, those good old times
Adventures they had in their lives
It's a wonder any one survived
The ladies sit there all the while
Quiet with a knowing smile
Not saying much agin or for
But when the men begin to snore
And just us girls we are alone
Well, we have stories of our own!

Natures lessons

We can learn a lot from nature. If we listen and pay attention. Not only to what we see and hear, but to what is, just there if we only take the time to see it. Nature and God's creatures will teach us not only how to live, but how to live together.

<u>Lessons from Nature</u>

If we listen to God's creatures
We find they are amazing teachers
You rarely see a stressed out cat
Or for that fact a sunburned bat
Squirrels know to plan ahead
And are never short a safe warm bed
A momma bear cares for her babies
Protects them, no ifs ands or maybes
Unconditional love, most folks can't reach it
And yet a good kind dog can teach it
Yet some people tear others to pieces
And we call ourselves the wiser species?

A summer storm

A mighty crash, a streak of light
There will be no sleep for me this night
While lying in my bed so warm
I am wakened by a summer storm
The lightning flashes split the night
And turn the world from dark to light
Followed by the Thunders roar
And then the sound of a downpour
Tomorrows plans go down the drain
Washed away by pouring rain
For with this storm, the coming day
Won't be one for making hay

Seasons

A single leaf falls like a tear
As the fall begins this year
Summer days come to an end
And the fall begins again
The colors change overnight
And reflect their beauty in the light
The Canada geese, heed the call
And gather up to fly each fall
The grasses change from green to brown
And we feel the chill as sun goes down
The critters they will now prepare
With thicker coats and longer hair
For winter's long and powerful reign
As this years end, comes again
With the cool and fading light
we know our world will soon be white
Fall and winter too will go
And with the melting of the snow
Renewed reborn the joy it brings
With the coming of the spring
We mark 4 seasons here each year
As one moves on the next appears
In life as well, the changes clear
As a single leaf, falls like a tear

What would you do

If you saw someone needing
on any given day
Would you reach out a hand? or
just turn away?
Would you question the right to be who they are
would you step up and help
or frown from afar
Would you leap straight to
judgement
without asking why
assume they are failing,
from failing to try
When you see someone needing
what would you do
ask yourself now
if that someone was you ?

Heartbeats

Poems of life, heartfelt thoughts and ponderings. Not specific to country life, but somehow still very much a glimpse of my life.

Will you be there?

When your burdens in life,
Become too heavy to bear
Call out to me, I will be right there
To reach out my hand, to help you along
To listen to you, and to pray and be strong
The weight of our world is too often too much
But so easily balanced with a kind heart and touch
A shoulder to lean on, a warm hand to hold
A comfort like a blanket, brings you in from the cold
When your burdens are lightened,
And you are rested again
Life moving forward, to the light again
Tell me this one thing
It is only fair
When my burdens get heavy
Will you be there?

<u>Live life by living it</u>

It hurts sometimes, this life of mine
but I wouldn't change it ,
not one time
The bumps the stings, the aches and pains
It cost far less than what I gained
We can live our lives and ride the ride
or wait and watch and let it slide
I come from tough and stubborn stock
we do the work , not talk the talk
When each day ends I take my rest
and hope I was equal to each test
Live life by living every day
don't wait and let it slip away
Fear can hold you back its true
but don't let it take on all of you
Breathe the air and dance the dance
And give this life you live a chance

Smiles

Take the time
Once in a while
To just be the reason
For a stranger to smile
Give them your hand
Open the door
Or offer some shelter
From a downpour
In a world that's so busy
And hustling about
Our minds become selfish
We never look out
But take just a moment
Now and again
To open our hearts
And let kindness shine in
If each of us took on
This one little task
What could we gain?
Do you have to ask?
A little more joy and peace
To be found
And many more smiles
If you look around
But please don't forget
To keep it on track
When they smile at you
You smile right back

To be free

I watched some children play today
I watched while I was on my way
To fix a tire and another task
I stopped myself, just to ask
Were we ever free like that?
Could we ever play like that?
Before we weighed down with this and that
Were we ever free like that?
A child's joy, seen through adult eyes
Brings a tear, there is no surprise
The joy and abandon that they share
Seems lost to us in a world of care

For just today I close my eyes
And fly on a swing to reach the sky
Or slide on a slide, just in my mind
And leave the grownup world behind
For with the sun tomorrow will bring
Reality with its own sting
Worries and trials, we face each day
Leaves such little time to play
Shackles of this life it seems,
Takes up all our time and dreams
Hard work and, toil is where it's at
But oh! Just to be free like that!

As we grow older

As we grow older
And wiser and bolder
The years passing
Often too soon
Don't hide from your birthday
It isn't your worst day
Don't spend it alone in your room
Nothing to hide from
Just look what you have done
There really is no need to mourn
Let the people who love you
And the lord God above you
Rejoice for the day you were born!

<u>Do you think you know me well?</u>

Funny you can never tell

If what you see is all for real

Or what part of me do I conceal

A laugh a smile

A ready joke

Tough as nails

Or is it smoke

All brave and strong

Is what I sell

But take a look beneath the shell

A tender heart, so easily broken
By hurtful things, both done and spoken
I cover well, don't share my fears
And I try hard not to show my tears
If you take a second glance,
Look deeper now, and take a chance
See all of me, both good and bad
The heart you never knew I had

My Christmas wish

I will make a wish this Christmas Eve
For all to give and to receive
I promise I won't wish for very much
Just all creatures to have a loving touch
That joy and comfort and peace are shared
That shelter abounds and lives are spared
That family rejoice for loved ones come home
That no one is left afraid and alone
That no one is hungry, or out on the cold
I will wish for this, If I may be bold
It may not seem possible this gift to receive
But it can happen, I have to believe
For all to be loved, and kept warm and safe
This is what I wish, in continuing faith.

In this New Year

I do resolve

To take the problems

I cannot solve

And look them over quietly

And see if they truly

Belong to me

If they do, I'll take a shot

And really give it all I have got

To sort it out

And get it right

But I'll lose no more sleep at night

Over issues I truly cannot fix

Within my little bag of tricks

I will still give, and help

Where I can

But finally I understand

The best help that I can be

Is to learn to

Take care of me

Two hearts two hands

Two lives entwined
May you forever keep in mind?
The vows you said upon this day
And not let pride get in the way
Talk to each other
And listen well
Let your hearts sing with the wedding bells
Love and faith and patience too
Let them be strong in both of you
Celebrate each passing year
With love together
And without fear
The handsome groom, the bride in white
My wish for you,
A future bright

A sparkling ring does mark the start

As a journey begins, two hands one heart
Vows you will repeat upon that day
Listen closely to what you say
Those promises you make each other
Are bound by love above no other
As in life's journey you will find
Those words are good to keep in mind
Life is not always hearts and flowers
But love and faith, have incredible powers
And when you have been married many years
Lived together through joys and tears
Look back upon this day you shared
And celebrate because you dared
To commit your selves to one another
Bound in love above no other

My heroes haven't always been cowboys!

These final few poems celebrate the ladies! The unsung heroes of the country, who do the work, and hold home and family together with grace love and good old determination! To my sister, Mother, Grandmothers, Aunts, and the friends I call sisters of my heart, I salute you!

For my sister

Here is a story I will share
A lovely girl
With raven hair
A vibrant and a daring child
This girl was never meek and mild
She grew up daring, but not too wild
Kind of heart and fair of face
And found her calling
With God's grace
A mother strong and full of love
A teacher, and mentor, giver of
Hope and home and abiding love
Where is this beauty
Can you see her?
Of course you can
She is in
Your mirror.

Daughters of the land

A daughter of the land
She will understand
When dinner is a few hours late
She will leave it to warm
And head out on the farm
And push the loose stock through the gate
If there is work to be done, she is the one
Who is out there right alongside you
Not afraid to get dirty, even if it ain't Purdy
She will do just what she needs to
Now don't you laugh, she will carry a calf
That needs her without any question
To just let it lie, and possibly die
Is an Impossible suggestion
She is stubborn and strong
And will work the day long
With not even so much as a thank you
For that is just how she was taught to
She has a heart that is tender
So please do remember
She's human and your words can hurt her
Though she will never show it
Or let you know it,
The damage is only too clear
Don't think you are above her
Let her alone or just love her
It's her choice,
She should be allowed
She lives for her family; she is all she can be
And her wish is to make them proud

For the wild ones

Before we hurt,
Before we were scared
When we took life flat out
Just because we were dared
Jumped into the water
Not thinking disaster
The current was strong
And we just swam faster

The horses we rode,
The stories we told
The chances worth taking
We were fearless and bold

Up till the wee hours
Always home late
Chores done at six
At work by eight!

So why did we stop
Did we really get smarter?
Or was keeping that pace,
Just getting harder?

Now don't you worry
She is still there inside
A little bit tired
But she hasn't died
Once in a while
If the timing is right
She'll howl at the moon
And dance through the night

So here's to the wild ones
Wherever they are
I'll drink a toast to us
Out under the stars!

70

Now I will bid you farewell. I wish you joy and happiness on your continuing path and leave you with the reminder, that anything is possible! It just might take some "figuring"

Thank you

Sherry